THE NATURE KIDS GUIDE TO

HEDGEHOGS

DAVID ANDERSON

LP Media Inc. Publishing
Text copyright © 2026 by LP Media Inc.
All rights reserved.

For information address LP Media Inc. Publishing,
30012 Variolite St NW, Princeton MN 55371
www.lpmedia.org

Publication Data

Hedgehogs
The Nature Kid's Guide to Hedgehogs — First edition.

Summary: "Learn all about Hedgehogs, the Nature Kid Way"
— Provided by publisher.

ISBN: 979-8-89818-113-0

[1. Hedgehogs – Non-Fiction] I. Title.

Title: The Nature Kid's Guide to Hedgehogs

CONTENTS

HEDGY HOMES

Hedgehogs often make their nests at the base of thick hedges. This is how they got their name. A hedge is a row of bushes where these animals often hide.

Snuffle! A hedgehog pokes its nose out from dry leaves.

Hedgehogs need cozy places to live. They like spots with bushes, tall grass, and piles of leaves. Some live where it is warm and dry. Others live where it is cool and damp.

These small animals look for safe spots to sleep. They hide under bushes, rock piles, and fallen logs. Hedgehogs build nests from grass and leaves. They tuck the soft bits into cozy piles.

A good nest keeps a hedgehog warm and dry. Each hedgehog finds its own special spot to call home.

WORLD WANDERERS

Rustle! A hedgehog crawls through tall grass. It sniffs the air for bugs.

Hedgehogs live in Europe, Asia, and Africa.

European hedgehogs live in England. They live in France, Germany, and many other countries.

Long-eared hedgehogs live in Russia and China.

African pygmy hedgehogs live in central Africa.

Desert hedgehogs live in Egypt. They live in Saudi Arabia too. Indian hedgehogs live in India and Pakistan.

No wild hedgehogs live in North America or Australia.

There are seventeen different species of hedgehogs living around the world.

TINY TROTTERS

Squeak! A tiny hedgehog fits in a person's hand. It is small and light!

Hedgehogs are small animals. Most weigh less than two pounds. That is only a little heavier than a baseball!

These animals have short, round bodies. Most measure five to twelve inches long. They also have tiny tails that are hard to see.

Some hedgehogs are even smaller than others. The long-eared hedgehog is one of the smallest kinds. It can weigh less than one pound.

A hedgehog's prickly spines make up about one third of its total body weight!

SPIKY SUITS

DID YOU KNOW?
Hedgehog spines are smooth, not barbed like porcupine quills. They are not sharp enough to stick in skin.

Crunch! A hedgehog curls tight. Its spines stick out everywhere.

Hedgehogs have thousands of spines on their backs. Each spine is a stiff, hollow hair that feels sharp and pointy.

Spines cover the top of a hedgehog. But the belly has soft fur instead. The face also has fur, not spines.

Over time, hedgehogs slowly lose and replace their spines. Each spine grows old, falls out, and a new spine grows in its place. Baby hedgehogs' first spines appear within hours of being born.

SUPER
SNIFFERS

Sniff! A hedgehog moves its wet nose side to side.

Hedgehogs have an amazing sense of smell. Their noses help them find food in the dark. They can smell bugs hiding underground.

Hedgehogs also hear very well. Their ears pick up tiny sounds. They can hear insects moving nearby.

Their eyesight is not as strong. Hedgehogs can see shapes but not fine details. They rely on their other senses more than their sight.

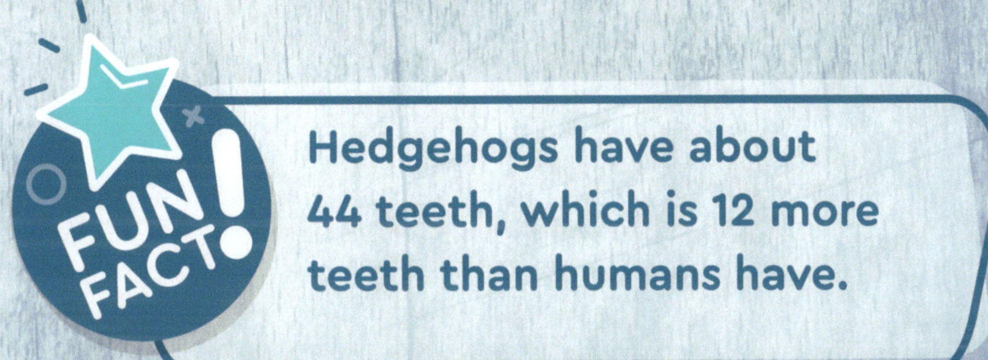

Hedgehogs have about 44 teeth, which is 12 more teeth than humans have.

PRICKLY
PROTECTION

Poke! A hedgehog's sharp spines point up at a curious fox.

Hedgehog spines are great for defense. When danger comes near, the spines stand up. This makes the hedgehog look big and scary.

Each spine has a sharp tip. It can poke a predator's nose or mouth. Most **predators** do not want to bite something so pointy!

Hedgehogs have strong back muscles. These muscles pull the spines tight. The spines form a wall.

A typical hedgehog has about five thousand to seven thousand spines on its body.

BUG BUFFET

Chomp! A hedgehog bites into a crunchy beetle. It is time for dinner.

Hedgehogs eat many kinds of bugs. They munch on beetles. They eat caterpillars and **earwigs** too. Hedgehogs also eat slugs and snails. But they often like beetles best.

All these bugs give hedgehogs energy. One hedgehog can eat dozens of insects in one night.

Hedgehogs eat other foods too. They nibble on fallen fruit. They eat bird eggs. Some hedgehogs even catch frogs or small mice.

Hedgehogs even eat millipedes, which many animals avoid.

SNIFF IT OUT

Hedgehogs can hear high-pitched sounds that humans cannot hear. This helps them find tiny insects in the grass.

Scratch! A hedgehog digs in soft dirt. It found a tasty worm hiding below.

Hedgehogs hunt by using their noses. They walk slowly and sniff the ground. Their noses twitch as they search for food.

When a hedgehog smells something tasty, it starts digging. Its small paws scratch at dirt and leaves. It pushes its snout into the soil.

Hedgehogs lick and taste things too. This helps them decide if something is good to eat. Then they grab worms with their mouths.

Some hedgehogs look under rocks and logs. Bugs often hide in these dark spots, so the hedgehog gobbles them up quickly.

WATCH OUT

Growl! A hungry badger sniffs near a hedgehog den.

Hedgehogs have many enemies. Badgers are their biggest predators. They have long claws that can unroll a curled hedgehog.

Owls also hunt hedgehogs. They swoop down from above at night. Eagle owls are large enough to catch them.

Foxes sometimes try to eat hedgehogs, but spines often stop them. Most foxes give up and walk away.

Some large birds grab young hedgehogs. Hoglets have softer spines.

Snakes sometimes try to eat hedgehogs. But swallowing all those spines is nearly impossible!

ROLL UP

Snap! A hedgehog hears danger. In a flash, it rolls into a tight ball.

When scared, hedgehogs curl up. They tuck their head and legs inside. Their body becomes a spiky ball.

Strong muscles pull the skin tight. This helps keep the ball shape firm. The spines point out in all directions.

Most predators cannot bite through. If they try, the spines poke their nose and mouth. Many animals just walk away.

A hedgehog can stay curled in a ball for hours until it feels safe again.

WADDLE WALK

Thump! A hedgehog waddles across a garden path. Its little legs work hard.

Hedgehogs have short legs, so they walk with a waddle. Their round bodies sway side to side.

Hedgehogs move slowly most of the time. They take small steps on flat feet.

When scared, hedgehogs can run faster. They trot quickly to find a hiding spot. At night, they can even run for miles!

Hedgehogs are surprisingly good swimmers and can paddle across ponds and streams when they need to.

NIGHT SHIFT

Hoot! The sun sets, and a hedgehog wakes up and stretches.

Hedgehogs are **nocturnal**. This means they are active at night. They sleep during the day in nests or burrows.

At dusk, hedgehogs wake up hungry. They spend hours searching for food in the dark. Their keen noses help guide them.

Night is safer for small animals. Fewer predators are awake. By dawn, hedgehogs return to their nests.

A hedgehog can walk two miles in one night! Their amazing noses help them find bugs in the dark.

27

SOLO STROLLERS

Hush! A hedgehog walks alone through the quiet garden.

Hedgehogs live alone most of the time. They do not form groups or packs. Their home areas may overlap with other hedgehogs.

They walk by themselves at night. One hedgehog may meet another. They sniff each other. Then they move on.

Hedgehogs only come together to mate. Then they live alone again.

Hedgehogs recognize each other by smell. Each one has its own unique scent marker.

FINDING FRIENDS

Grunt! Two hedgehogs meet under a bush. They sniff each other to say hello.

Hedgehogs find each other by smell. Males follow scent trails left by females.

When a male finds a female, he circles around her. He may do this for hours. The female often huffs and puffs at him.

After mating, hedgehogs go separate ways. The male does not help raise babies. Instead, each hedgehog returns to living alone.

Baby hedgehogs are called hoglets. A mother hedgehog usually has four to five hoglets at a time.

HOGLETS HERE

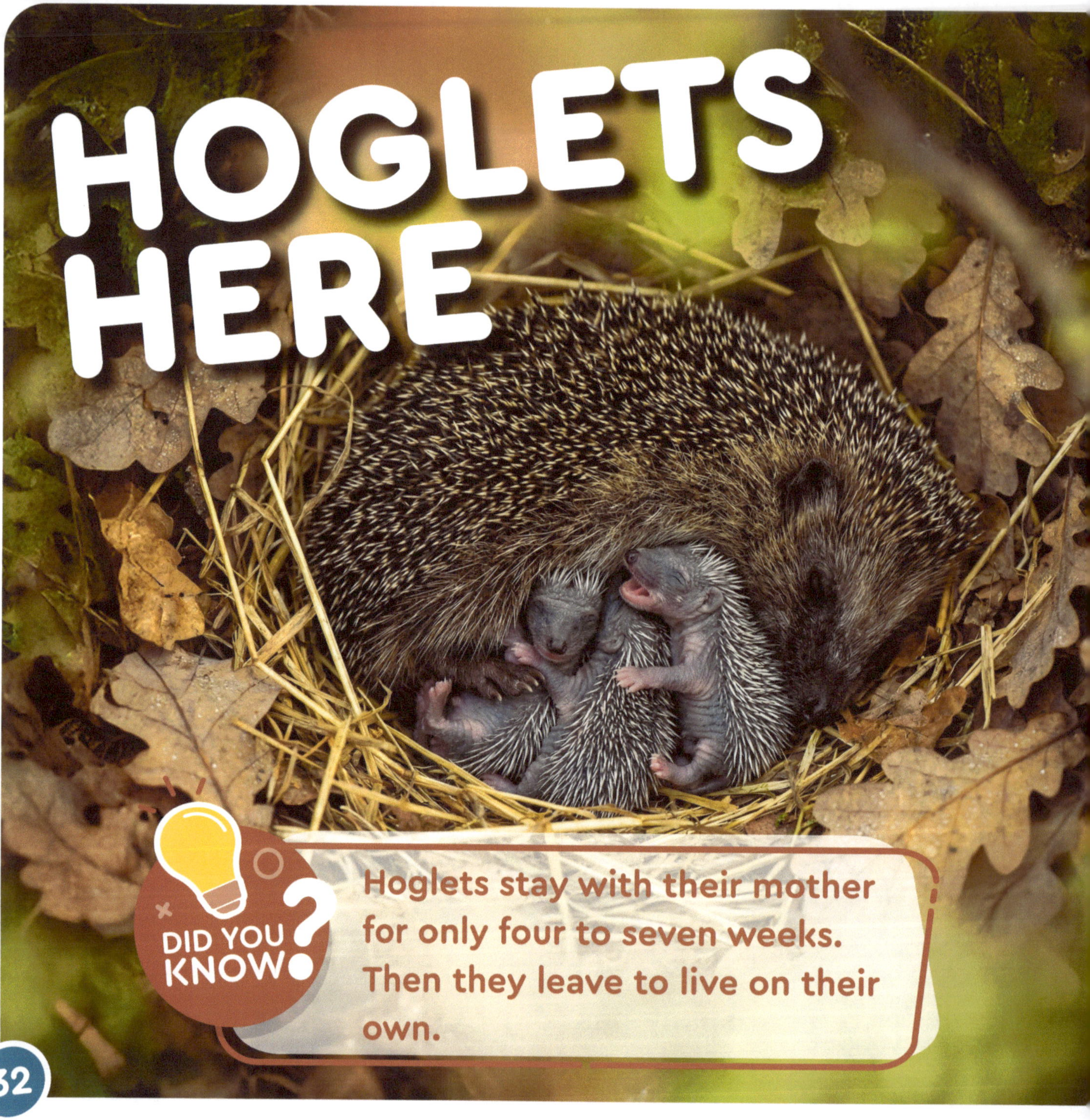

Hoglets stay with their mother for only four to seven weeks. Then they leave to live on their own.

Chirp! Newborn hoglets snuggle close in their leafy home.

Baby hedgehogs are called **hoglets**. These tiny babies are born blind and deaf. A mother usually has four to five hoglets at once.

Newborn hoglets have about 100 white spines hidden under their skin. Within hours, the spines pop out and harden.

Hoglets grow fast. Their eyes open after about two weeks, and they start exploring outside the nest at about four weeks old.

MOM KNOWS BEST

Snort! A mother hedgehog carries leaves to her nest.

Mother hedgehogs raise hoglets alone. They build warm nests before giving birth. This keeps babies safe and hidden.

Mothers feed their hoglets milk for about six weeks. During the first four weeks, babies stay safe in the nest. If danger comes near, a mother may move her babies to a new spot.

Hoglets learn to find food by following their mother. After about six weeks, young hedgehogs leave to live on their own.

PRICKLY SUPERPOWERS

Snap! A hedgehog rolls into a tight ball.

By now you know that hedgehogs have about 5,000 quills on their backs. But did you know the quills are made of keratin, the same stuff your fingernails are made of?

Those quills do more than poke predators. If a hedgehog falls from a high place, the quills act like cushions. They can bounce and walk away without getting hurt!

Hedgehogs are immune to some snake venom. This helps them hunt and eat small snakes without getting sick.

HEDGEHOG PETS

Pet hedgehogs should not eat milk or bread. These foods can make them very sick.

Sniff! A pet hedgehog pokes its nose into soft dirt.

Many people keep hedgehogs as pets. They are quiet and fun to watch. They need a warm cage with soft bedding to sleep in.

Pet hedgehogs need fresh water each day. A shallow dish works best. Hedgehogs drink a lot!

Pet stores sell special hedgehog food. They also love treats like mealworms and crickets.

Pet hedgehogs need their nails trimmed just like dogs and cats. Long nails can curl and hurt their tiny feet.

GLOSSARY

earwigs
Small brown insects with pincers on their back end.

hoglets
Baby hedgehogs.

nocturnal
Active at night and sleeping during the day.

predator
An animal that hunts and eats other animals.

species
A group of animals that are the same kind.